SPLIT VERSE

POEMS TO HEAL YOUR HEART

Edited by Meg Campbell and William Duke

MIDMARCH ARTS PRESS
New York

To our Mothers,
Betsey and Ruth Mary

Acknowledgments

"Honeymoon" by Peter E. Murphy appeared in *Poultry, A Magazine of Voice*, Spring, 1987. "The Marriage" by Ellen Bryant Voigt appeared in *Claiming Kin*, Wesleyan University Press. "Some Places I've Driven From" by Larry Mallory appeared in *Potomac Review*. "The Best Sex" by William Duke appeared in *Saturn: A New York City Periodical*. "Still Life" by Lawrence Russ appeared in *Connecticut River Review*. "My Marriage" by Kelly Cherry appeared in *Relativity: A Point of View*, Louisiana State University Press. "Divorce Boxing" by D. C. Berry is in *Divorce Boxing*, Eastern Washington University Press. "Court Date," "The Way to Survive Divorce," and "To a Single Mother" by Meg Campbell appeared in *Solo Crossing*, Midmarch Arts Press, 1999. "Custody" by Maureen Flannery appeared in *Rambunctious Review*, Chicago, Illinois. "How We Came to Stand on That Shore" by Jay Rogoff appeared in *The Quarterly*. "Change of Address" by William Matthews appeared in *Blues If You Want*, Houghton Mifflin, 1989.

Library of Congress Catalog Card Number 00 130315
ISBN 1-877675-35-0

Printed in the United States of America

Published in 2000 by
Midmarch Arts Press
300 Riverside Drive
New York, New York 10025

Contents

Introduction

More people in more places across America are reading, writing, and listening to poetry today than ever before. They are writing poems in journals and with magnetic letters on their refrigerators. They are becoming poets. Some of them are also becoming divorced, and, when they do, poems pour forth about that difficult, complex experience. In *Split Verse*, new poets join well-respected veterans in this first-ever anthology on this challenging life experience.

Each divorce consists of a sequence of stages that must be passed through at one's own pace. Divorce is as particular as two people's thumbprints. Poems included here reflect this diversity of experience and points of view.

No one grows up wishing to become divorced, and children, except in the most abusive situations, always long for their parents to reconcile. But volcanoes do blow, tornadoes do strike, and the little fissures that begin early in marriage can become fault lines along which unexpected quakes occur.

The theme of *Split Verse* is resiliency in the face of trauma. Divorce is wrenching, not just for the spouses and children, but also the network of extended family, friends, and colleagues who are all impacted by what Kate Olmsted, herself the daughter of divorced parents, calls "family reorganization."

But why turn to poetry during divorce or when making sense of divorce? Even the most private grief may have a social dimension. Poetry is a way to share one's grief and make loss more bearable. Poetry gives voice to what is hidden in our hearts.

For some, divorce is a welcome relief. Yet it is never a happy, celebratory family event. Divorce is a failed marriage, and failure is something many of us have been taught to diminish or run from rather than face head-on and learn from. Paying close attention to divorce, there is much to learn about oneself, one's values, and about whom one loves and is loved by in a vulnerable, exposed time in one's life. Poetry, which may begin as the poet's tool for learning these lessons, can also be therapeutic for the reader.

Divorce offers a genuine chance to reengineer one's life. Poetry offers sustenance to our imagination as we summon courage to envision new lives.

Both of us turned to poetry at a time when our lives felt cracked open by divorce. It offered us a way to express the depth of denial, rage, pain, grief, and, in time, acceptance and growth that can accompany this momentous, unexpected journey. In the process, like many others, each of us found a new voice in poetry. When we looked up for air, we discovered hundreds of other poets also grappling with separation and divorce, and we invited them to submit poems to *Split Verse*.

These poems are like divorce. They prompt deep admiration of the human spirit in the most trying circumstances.

We believe you will triumph. It is in that spirit we share *Split Verse* with you.

Meg Campbell
Boston

William Duke
New York

MARRIAGE

HONEYMOON

Peter E. Murphy

All night,
We blast our wedding horns
In force.

And two years later
Quietly divorce.

THE EXCHANGE

Elizabeth Harrington

He is a man. He talks.
She is a woman. She listens.
He empties his pain
like small red plum tomatoes
into the waiting air.
The woman catches them
with outstretched palms.

Now the man is brown coffee that sobs.
He pours himself into the woman's eyes.
She nods and nods.
When he is empty he begins again.

Full of him, she sloshes with his story
and the problem of the can opener.
It's not working again.

Wordlessly she begins to clean his house,
sorting the junk into piles.
Buttons, brown shoelaces,
a red pin cushion
with the pins still in it.

The clutter begins to disappear
into meaningful piles.
She feels better and better.
But the attic is in her head,

you know, and although he sees it
he doesn't understand.

When the sun spreads its butter,
one of them is missing.
And the piles have disappeared, too.
Not a single object is left.

But if you added water to the woman,
she would fill up and expand till her stomach split.
And her sorrow would astound you
with its variety of colors and sounds
and the oddly shaped things

that spill from it: a bird feeder,
a shepherd's crook,
some wind chimes that would make you
turn your head if you could hear them.
But of course you never could.

THE MARRIAGE

Ellen Bryant Voigt

Under its angry skin, her grief
ripens: succulent, wound-color.
She knew there were other women —
his baroque excuses for silence —
but knew in the weaker hemisphere
of her heart, that stringent
muscle pumping in, valve opened.
Hinged clam, living for fifteen years
on grit and gravel, housed now against
the weather, she has the car, the kids,
an appetite for garbage. He's got
a new wife, wants her to take him in,
produce a pearl.

THE BEST SEX

William Duke

I want to hear your smoky voice
and see you smile at me
with those full-bottle-of-cabernet eyes
that say you're ready.
Ready for bed.
Ready for me to kiss you deeply in the mouth.
Ready for me to gently run my tongue
across your closed eyelids.
Unbuttoning blouse,
breathing hot whispers of "oooh" in your ear
before making slow journey down your smooth neck
and sucking each swelling breast and each pink nipple
till they're hard and ripe as berries.
I want to listen to your engine purr like a limo on the freeway
as my mouth moves down your arching torso
stopping briefly to tongue your navel and nip inside each
pale thigh before
reaching over and spreading your wet labia apart
and lapping your brackish sex like
a thirsty dog in summer heat.
Lapping love sounds like water lapping on shore
over and over
like waves of northeaster foaming on rising tide
modulating tempo, continue till I feel your sex
grow large and soft
and your alabaster abdomen rises in orgasm
and you tell me you are.
Writhing beneath me, you'll stretch like a panther and
I'll turn you over and mount you from behind
and feel the skin of your ass as soft as milk.
I'll thrust in and out through a history of pleasure —
you a sphinx with head down dampening desert

with tears of ecstasy and passion cries echoing through ages
connected like all animals before us.
You'll reach your right hand back and scratch my balls until
I explode with blinding truth and beauty.
Then I'll fall down on top of your back
exhausted and limp
with the understanding that we have the best sex
when I don't look you in the eyes.

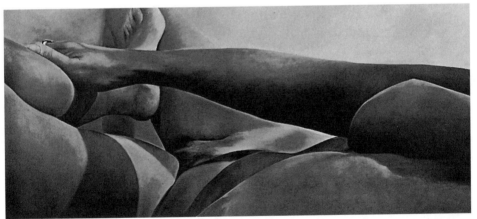

Joan Semmel, *Triangular Tunnels*, 1976; private collection

NEAR HERON LAKE

Kim Addonizio

During the night, horses passed close
to our parked van. Inside I woke cold
under the sleeping bag, hearing their heavy sway,
the gravel harsh under their hooves as they moved off
down the bank to the river. You slept on,
though maybe in your dream you felt them enter
our life just long enough to cause that slight
stirring, a small spasm in your limbs and then
a sigh so quiet, so close to being nothing
but the next breath, I could believe you never guessed
how those huge animals broke out of the dark and came
toward us. Or how afraid I was before I understood
what they were — only horses, not anything
that would hurt us. The next morning
I watched you at the edge of the river
washing your face, your bare chest beaded with bright water,
and knew how much we needed this,
the day ahead with its calm lake
we would swim in, naked, able to touch again.
You were so beautiful. And I thought
the marriage might never end.

WHEN THE WIFE SLAMS A COFFEE CUP ON A TABLE IN THE WILDERNESS OF THE HUSBAND'S HEAD, DOES IT MAKE A SOUND?

Frank Van Zant

Husband's bland response *yes, it was raining, but we didn't cancel practice because you know they have to compete rain or shine* carries layers of history, the wife thinking of husband as selfish, team-first, even punishing, thinking of her hours with the kids, added-to, unending, with kids to wake, kids to dress, kids to feed, kids in every moment of her sublimated soul whispering how all she does, she does for someone else, never her first, never with some championship to win, so that in her lowering cup is a staring moment
her
husband saying d*arling, because it's raining I'm home, so please go out, be free for a time,*

get a makeover at Sassoon's, take a weekend at Aruba, dance incautiously with wild island men, drink carnal margaritas the cup sounding with hope for what the husband might hear.

SOME PLACES I'VE DRIVEN FROM

Larry Mallory

The land here lies flat beneath the sky.
Any mountains will be supplied
by memory. Some places leave you

wrapped in ribbons. In others
you lay open. It is all much the same.
Innocent roads have claimed many lives.

Not far from here there's a cemetery
full of poets. In the morning
we sit on the patio and drink coffee

spiked with last night's argument.
The fat man mows the lawn. He's already
grumbled politics and there's nothing

left to do but cut the grass. We agree,
there's hardly ever an escape. I lay
my book on my lap and think road.

DOWN SOUTH WITH SOMEONE ELSE AS THE MARRIAGE NEARS THE END

Charles Rossiter

fragrance tornadoes the window
the clock runs wild and late
last light bombards the wall

wind blows uncertain
three trees creak
like a rusted iron gate

old guilts hung out on a line
like a maze of left-over lace
a cascade of kudzu on the telephone wires

the half-closed door
swings slowly on its hinges
moonlight expands and contracts

the comfort of stars
ironic smiles
cornstalks in generic confusion

a horse tugs at a ragged tether
till it breaks and he shambles off
blue morning lies down

NOTE THIS

Lisa Allen Ortiz

Because your face came at me like a fist, and because you tore
into my bedroom with Dionysian delight, wrecking
everything to make me drunk and then left me crazy and
naked, torn apart by wild horses, my heart transformed into a
bird beating wildly in the bereaved cage of my chest and
because your maenad friends trampled my yard into a grotto
of treachery and riot and because you raged into the night
and asked me endless riddles, and because I am inflamed by
wine and religious ecstasy and because I bludgeoned my own
soul with an ax and have grown barren at the horror of such a
crime and because I know this is
really
truly
love
I am asking you
to please
please
leave now.

SEEING IN THE DARK

Peter Desey

Twenty-five years sharing
the same bed, table and skins,
their bodies revolted
finally, stripped of their mysteries,
naked and familiar as the furniture
and the worn paths on the carpet.
One more night of passing headlights
sweeping the ceiling of the bedroom
seemed too much for eyes
to follow, and she got up
and picked at the frayed arms
of the brown sofa and began to cry
because dishes and the lamps
were so exactly there. He lay away,
his hands at his sides
on the sheets, thin cover for
the August night. Rooms apart,
they thought sometime they might
sleep and dream again in vivid
images of flesh and of a secret,
what they would become.
There must be more than this.

Lisa Zwerling, *Couple VIII*; private collection

SEPARATION

HAIKU #49

Kalamu ya Salaam

thought I left you but
my train rumbles in circles
each station is you.

WANDERING HOME

Judith Dickerman-Nelson

My husband and I drive through two states —
New Hampshire, Vermont — and for the first time
since our separation, I've begun to believe
there is something we can return to. We climb

mountains, pass over town borders, the distance
between exits growing as we move farther
north. The farmland rolls beside the highway,
and it seems there are more cows than cars —

we count heifers like Volkswagens, a new version
of a childhood game. My husband points out
two cows too far from any farmhouse and wonders how
they got so lost, saying they must have wandered, but

I argue for a barn outside of our vision,
just over the next hill, and say the cows will
find their haven, though I am afraid and pray
they can smell the path leading home, still.

SEPARATION

Susan Richardson

We could have been New Zealand's
Rangi and Pap, your vast rational sky,
my rich creative earth, our daughter
pushing up between us, a natural divider,
her hands the roots of a tree,
legs and feet in the air, full-blossoming.

Like the Greeks Rhea and Cronos,
their sons haggling for power,
wrenching sky from earth,
a necessary upheaval, historical,
the terrible twos, adolescent rebellion —

Between us now:
space to roam,
air to breathe,
and, when we wish it,
your falling rain,
my rising mist.

THE SEPARATION

Bruce Taylor

The morning,
this miracle,
we kiss and stir
surface, drift
back gradually
into reach.

We part as lips
do, after kissing,
toss back and forth
an uncommitted wave.

Let go, we say, to whom
we're not certain.
Let go, we say, but
why we don't know.

I go up and over
the hill I live on,
the other side of
now it's far enough.
You stay there,
so close.

YOU RIPPED OUT THE IVY

William Duke

On a gray day
drops fall silently in the garden.
The dampness softens the bright verdant leaves
of ivy in early spring
hanging limp and heavy, thick and lush
still but still growing with phosphorescent edges
a hearty plant, wild
a miracle of adaptation to our urban ecosystem
romantic and wonderful overgrown in our garden
but "it is a weed," you said
it had to go, though I said "no."
The first year while I was out you removed half of it
and planted boxwood and azalea in its place.
I don't believe you did it, against my will.
I cried that day.
You said I was ungrateful for the work and the expense you
went to.
You ripped out the ivy for the promise of dry soil
and pot-bound plants brought in from Long Island.
It made me smile when the bushes turned brown from
dryness and neglect and when the naked dirt eroded and
clogged the drains.
The next spring you brought in Liz
"'cause you don't do anything to help around here,"
you said and you both ripped out the rest
and planted more bushes in neat little rows.
Only a small patch of ivy was left when I came home.
It circled the base of our dead tree
and climbed halfway up its hollow trunk.
I don't believe you ripped out all the fucking ivy

and stuffed it with my heart in Hefty trash bags for removal
to the curb.
You must have felt stronger about it than I did,
or my inaction was no match for your cruel action.
"Could you please haul it out,
'cause you don't do anything to help around here,"
you said.
On a gray day
drops fall silently in the garden without ivy.
It's your garden now.

FOR THE SAKE OF THE BODY

Gianna Russo

But this is a useless ritual.
On the pillow it always rejects, I place my head
and offer myself to the sleep god, the set punishment of denial.
I settle back and ass onto the comforter, which is mute
and offers no reassurances.
I calm my belly into the earned slackness of a mother's body.
I take out my breasts until they are easy.
I let my feet turn away from themselves
and rest on the meager sympathies of the mattress
like both sides of the argument for my life:
the one I think I have, the one I think I want.
I uncurl my hands, which have held all and nothing,
and stretch out my arms, which have reached for everything.
I loosen the muscles in my neck.
Between the minor consolations of headboard and footboard
I open my legs to some small goodness,
the meeting place of my hands.
Although every cell is swollen with the loss of you,
I try to lay down this outmoded will.
Still, the bedposts salute four ways to promise nothing.

MOONLIGHT, NIGHT SWEATS, AND MADNESS

Jeanne Lutz

Brighter than the sun,
the moonlight wakes her.
Turning over she admits
he's gone and the empty
place on the other side of the bed
is his.

Night sweats.

By the blue glow and open
window, she lies on his side, her body
casting a shadow onto her side
of the bed, still damp
as she wonders what will happen
if she tries to take his place — be manly,

be aggressive. She wonders
if her shadow, cast by blue-white
light will be enough of him
to be her.

RANT OF THE RECENTLY SEPARATED

Peter Wade

I wish I could yell at you but my anger has turned inward to what my shrink calls a depression.

My serotonin re-uptake inhibitor is keeping me from giving a shit about all the fucked up things you've done to destroy what was a reasonably functional life.

I'm really pissed that you're unfazed and smile back at me in your white wine and Atavan daze and pretend that we're friends for the sake of the fucking kids! You even pretend that you and Mike are friends for the sake of the fucking kids! Fuck Mike!

You look at me with those I'm-so-sorry-for-you eyes, and it makes me want to scream, but I look back and pretend it's cool. I even had dinner and polite conversation with you at Julie's birthday and all the while you smiled at me with the condescending sympathy of an outplacement counselor.

My only solace is found in my penis and my new girlfriend, or transitional object, as my shrinks call her. But the fucking Prozac is making it harder for me to perform. Even still she's much better in bed than you ever were!

I get up and go to work and try to concentrate on business but business sucks. I tried positive thinking but people thought I was crazy.

I spend my evenings riding the subways to my therapists. I have two, one for medication and one for feelings. My medicine man wants to know if my ejaculatory response is too long and if I'm getting any other side effects from the Prozac. My feelings doctor wants to know why I can't get mad at you.

I pull it together every other weekend for the kids, but they know I'm a basket case. I can barely remember their birthdays. The little one beats me up worse than you did. She learned it from you. The older one makes an effort to be kind but is scared 'cause the little one runs the show and it is terrifying to know that a six-year-old has more power than your daddy.

The family's fallen apart ever since you became bored. Ever since you had to make out with Alan Buckfinger and you became infatuated with Mike, who no longer works at your firm so you can go hiking with him in Montana. You can be sensitive with each other. Maybe he'll even tolerate the sappy songs from Bonnie Raitt that you used to put on loud when you were half loaded and wanted to screw. I hope so, 'cause I don't give a flying fuck!

When I'm not at my shrinks' I go to poetry readings. It's the only place I can go where the people are as fucked up as I am.

STILL LIFE

Lawrence Russ

The plate lies in pieces where it fell.
And you've stopped watering the plants:
the wandering Jew no longer wanders
toward the carpet, the fern in its hanging pot
turns brown and stiff.

Things that should have kept us together
show up now, fixed in their places,
like suits and dresses, scarves and gloves,
in the darkened windows
of stores closed for the night.

Marian Lerner Levine, *Still Life on Geometric Lace*, 1980; courtesy of the artist

HAIKU #10

Kalamuya Salaam

patient, you wait but
I'm gone, a flung stone sadly
sinking in water.

BREAKING UP IS HARD TO DO

Katherine McAlpine

The one who chose to walk away
may also grieve and feel bereft,
wakens to tears of bleak dismay,
facing a terrifying cleft.
But this is better, any day,
than being the person who was left.

BLOODMOBILE

Mary Scott

The technician rests
my left arm on the computer,
notices my naked ring finger
two days after I removed
my wedding band, a strip of flesh
depressed and colorless as tripe.

What happened here? he probes.
I tell him I'm separated,
saying it aloud for the first time.
He says he's sorry, he knows
how it feels.

Then he takes my hand
like an injured animal
he's removed from the road
and lances my fingertip.
It doesn't even bleed.

DIVORCE

THE DIVORCEE AND GIN

Kim Addonizio

I love the frosted pints you come in,
and the tall bottles with their uniformed men;
the bars where you're poured chilled
into shallow glasses, the taste of drowned olives,
and the scrawled benches where I see you
passed impatiently from one mouth
to another, the bag twisted tight around
your neck, the hand that holds you
shaking a little from its need,
which is the true source of desire. God, I love
what you do to me at night when we're alone,
how you wait for me to take you into me
until I'm so confused with you I can't
stand up anymore. I know you want me
helpless, each cell whimpering, and I give
you that, letting you have me just the way
you like it. And when you're finished
you turn your face to the wall while I curl
around you again, and enter another morning
with aspirin and the useless ache
that comes from loving, too well,
those who, under the guise of pleasure,
destroy everything they touch.

MY MARRIAGE
(Genus: Lepidodendron)

Kelly Cherry

It goes under like a spongy log,
soaking up silica.

I love these stony roots
planted in time, these stigmaria,

this scaly graduate
of the school of hard knocks,

these leaf-scarred rocks
like little diamonds.

And the rings! . . . the rings
and cells that show forth

clearly, fixed and candid
as the star in the north.

Giant dragonflies, corals,
the tiny bug-eyed trilobite

grace this paleosite
with shell and wing, cool,

amberstruck exoskeleton,
nice flash of improbability

felled and stuck, past
petrified in present, free

from possibility's hard and arbitrary
demands. Once, seed ferns swooned,

languid as the currents in a lost lagoon,
while warm winds swarmed over the damp earth

like locusts and rain was manna.
I hold that time still.

Divorce keeps it real and intact,
like a fossil.

RECONCILIATION

Meg Files

We meet in this foreign cafe outside
in the foreign spring where dun birds
hum and unknown trees, thin
and purple-sheathed, drip blossoms, and we
point to items on the menu, understanding
nothing. Believe me, this is not France, no
island, nowhere in the southern hemisphere.
We are shy. Do you like this? — tasting
hot green filling rolled in what is not tortilla
or chapati. We clink smoky glasses together.
Here's to — what? Who followed whom
to this land — out of our homeland
where politics as usual and our blue dishes
are quiescent in the cupboard? Customs
fall away. On the temples here the graven
animals have gray wings. Who runs
this place? What is the music? What of
tears? What do the denizens want?
In the homeland die our mothers,
appaloosa fathers, our boy. We
cannot go there. Remote ruins, carved
with the ninety-nine names
for blame, fall away. Here they have
tender pronouns: him, her. What is
wild here, what cultivated? Here
at the ends of the earth? Here
where we are exiled, are clean.

SETTLEMENT

Gail White

Who gets custody of the bones
under the bed? he asked.
I do, she said. Community property.
You had no bones under the bed
when you married me.
Now just a minute, he said,
I earned them myself.
But I put you through school, she said,
and that gives me a stake.
Don't be so hard, he said.
Remember where we got that skull?
That was in Venice.
We were so much in love then.
I don't want to part with the skull,
it's full of memories.
You'll be lucky to get the femurs,
she said in a rage.
Don't try to soft-soap me,
you sonofabitch.
Listen! They're rattling, he said.
They've done it at night,
but not in the daytime before.
What, she laughed, are you still
afraid of the bones?
Oh yes, he said. Oh yes.

SETTLEMENT

Sherman Pearl

Simple surgery,
a few scissor snips and we're
separated at the thighs;
one more through the gloss
cuts our hands apart.
Now the link between our eyes
is severed — no blood
and little pain.
We're still smiling at each other
as the blades remove
my head from yours.
Cut loose, my grin splits the sky,
gives us equal share of blue
and half a cloud apiece.
Tearing the cloud does not
produce rain.
The operation ends and we're
divided down the middle.
My portion has
half a house in the background,
yours the other half
and look! on the lawn, midway
where we'd stood together,
half a child.

COURT DATE

Meg Campbell

It was our last date.
Sadness my mantle,
relief my veil.
Take the stand.
Tell the court
I agree my marriage,
two decades, two children,
irretrievably broken down.
I remember fifteen years ago
the blue car broke down
and you left it.
Never went back.
How you puzzled me.
Or when you sobbed in my arms,
If you knew me, you would leave me.
I never knew.
When you walked
out
same age, same month
your father walked
never looked back
I was bone certain
you would return.
Wake up from this nightmare.
You in love
with your masseuse.

Tell the court
the settlement
is just and fair.
I have not been coerced.
Judge leans forward
awaits my tear-streaked assent.
Clerk hands me water.
Voice unsteady
courtroom silence breaks.
Papers to sign
bend down
kiss top page.
Lipstick marking
good-bye
to myself
as a wife.

DISSOLUTION

Peter Desey

I can't remember
what incantation broke
us lawfully. Did we walk
three times around each other,
say words that were a spell,
throw glasses on the floor,
stamp on a document with our dirty feet?
I think we declared each other
legally dead. It was a private
and quiet affair, the judge asking us
if this marriage had no hope.
Did I say, "Your Honor, faith and charity
have busted too?" I almost did.
The courtroom was a church that day,
pews and aisles brightly polished,
immaculate as grace. All we lacked
was a salver passed, meager love
our only offering. From the railing we
could see the black sleeve move, the signing
of the document. Unblessed, we stood below,
and the judge rose and wished us well.

COMING HOME FROM THE DIVORCE

Peter Desey

Things take their insignificance
from this. When I open the door,
the house exhales its stale air at me.
The hall light burns
at low intensity. Under the table,
crumbs. And the oven, cold. Each room
silent as the pause after
a deep breath. All the plugs
pulled from their sockets. And dust
gathering on dust.

DIVORCE BOXING

D. C. Berry

Divorce boxing is when you whip
   yourself for failing the Better
or Worse promise. "I am a piece of lint,"

       you say, "I lied right there
         at the altar

     before the devil and preach.

        I stabbed

   God in the back with his

            own crucifix —

     I, I, I, I." Berate yourself,

    stomp your poisonous heart —

    feel free, you are in a closet

of just yourself, with no lights on,
no ringside yelling million-dollar bets,
no bow-ties caring if you lose or win.

So, cross your eyes and give yourself
that kung fu chop straight to the crotch,
  the root of all your trouble in the first

   place. You confused Romance
with Biology, didn't you? the wine
and candlelight for blind hormones.

   Call yourself names and kick
yourself, throw psychology uppercuts
   till you're silly as a whitecap

      tossing on the ocean.
Make a whole ocean of whitecaps,

knocking yourself around

till your stupidities
are an Atlantic of meringue,
till your mistakes

are a pie you swallow and smile.
You're not the only one who's thrown
in the towel. What's the big deal?

AT LEAST HALF THE MAN MY FATHER WAS

David Mark Speer

Some men age badly,
trying mightily to stave off the ravages of time,
becoming in manner and aspect more adolescent as the years
wear on.
The scramble to stay young beats out growing old gracefully.
Hands down, nine times out of ten,
Most guys would rather be an up-and-comer than an elder
statesman,
because the elder part is what everyone sees first.
The compulsion to race the clock takes on many forms,
all easily recognizable —
a man starts to notice gray coming in at the temples,
or hair coming out in clumps,
and then come the showy efforts to appear "with it" and
"happening," —
as if a 48-year-old on a motorbike is in any way
"happening" —
most guys are just trying not to turn into their fathers.

My most fervent wish
is to meet a woman with whom I could share just a little bit
of my life.
The inner part,
the boarded-up attics and padlocked hope chests that house
all my secrets.
Fall in love enough to love her when she's the mother of our
children.
Stay in love long enough
for the kids to remember my face,

my features, my brand of cigarettes.
Then get divorced and become an old guy
living in a town far away from my home,
writing letters to my son,
who now smokes my brand.

If I can't aspire to anything better —
And we all turn into our parents anyway —
I want to be at least half the man my father was.

NOTHING ELABORATE:
NOTHING CONTEMPORARY

Kimmika L.H. Williams

When the final paper came
legal document
unimportant it seemed
despite the blue
construction paper-like "chumpy"
they'd attached to the back,
lest it be thrown away
as junk mail.
I suppose.
One single piece of paper
concluded it.
The end of an era,
a long time,
years
living with a man I had called
my mate, spouse,
lover,
friend.
Now,
the paper is filed
in a drawer
between past and present
along with all our "other"
important papers —
the kids' birth certificates,
a duplicate social security card
and the insurance
that we could never (ever) keep up.

No more of his smells
to remind me;
no more picking up his underwear
from the bathroom floor;
no more rolled and balled socks
hiding under covers
at the foot of the bed
to confirm his presence.
Divorce in hand —
nothing elaborate,
nothing contemporary;
just,
I be!

DIVORCE

Charles Rossiter

we were
three weeks
together
somewhere
her husband
waved
a gun
when she
told him
but didn't fire
into the phone
I moved
out, out,
my first wife
was no good
for me and
emotions
make me
nervous
I barely
recall
the rest
that wife
my hair
in the shower
but the one
with the husband
with the gun
who one day
stopped

returning my calls
she is indelible
as birth
and Erika
my daughter
she was one
at the time
she was one
she was
one.

CHILDREN

DIVORCE
(*for my brother*)

Kristen Guggenheim

Hiding under overturned rowboats,
graveyard of winter vessels at the end of our street,
you pared flakes of gray paint
from the bowed roof, watching them
twirl past the hem of fog light.

I found you there
lying along the splintered edge,
assembling broken shells into neat piles
paying homage to abandoned homes
of strange, shy inhabitants.

Hot cheek pressed into cool November sand,
you drew the outline of your nose,
pointy corner of the nostril flared
like Father's when he leaves the house,
suitcase banging against the storm door —

THE DIVORCE

Daniel F. Kligman

Children, we are sorry
To dismember piecemeal
Our little home,
Its background
And your horizon
In its backyard.
And we are sorry
That our two voices
Will no longer melt
In your minds
At night,
When you sleep,
Into one voice
To guide you
Through the next day
And on.
And we are sorry
That there will be less time
For this and that
And much more travel
Here and beyond
To and from
And messages to bring.
Things to take;
And about the cat.
But we aren't sorry
That we brought you
Over the threshold of our place
To grow into the world
Flow in spaces between us
And that we, as a result,
Are no longer as lonely
As we once were
On a night we dreamt.

EVERY OTHER WEEKEND

Stephen L. Lyons

Here in summer's transience of airport terminals,
we pass our offspring back and forth.
And with each exchange they slip
forever into a space
that is neither mother nor father.
Two homes for every child.
More people to love them.
So we say, knowing this is the biggest lie,
knowing children are too flexible for their own good,
knowing that we can no longer offer
the protection of two.

Alternating Fridays on my street
good-byes and adjustments
hang in the air.
Suitcases line the stoops,
the medicines and loaded messages
relayed between unraveled marriages
with enough left unsaid to say it all.
At either home the modest debris of the displaced
stands forgotten: bright Crayolas, misplaced
gloves, a form from school "to be signed
by a parent or guardian."

We thought we would get it right
this time, thought we would beat
the matrimonial odds, but this is our legacy.
This is what we create,
these small remains of family,
the ease of letting go.

MIDNIGHT

Tony Gloeggler

You want no one to know
you're home alone. You sit
in the dark, listen to Miles blow
"All Blue" through headphones. Upstairs,

a party. A glass smashes,
laughter and salsa splash through cracks
in the ceiling. Bottle rockets shoot
lines of light past your window.

The phone rings. You listen
to your machine. "Happy New Year,
Daddy. Don't forget about the circus
next Saturday. I miss you Daddy."

You rewind the tape,
play it back twice.

TO A SINGLE MOTHER

Meg Campbell

You never forget,
always scanning, tracking,
like dogs who dream of running
& move their legs in sleep,
you always run, awake —

WHAT ABOUT THE CHILDREN?

Dovid P. Primack

Mother and Father argue at night.
Mother and Father argue all day.
Sometimes, when we are in bed, they are hissing.
Sometimes at parties they mingle apart.
Sometimes they shout at the top of their lungs.

Mother and Father both have their lawyers.
Mother and Father both have their days.
Sundays and each second holiday — Dad's turn.
Weekdays and Saturdays and birthdays are Mom's,
But Dad gets to come with a present and stay!

Mother and Father vie for affection.
Mother and Father give us too much.
Why are we hungry for something forgotten?
Aren't the gifts and the outings enough?
I am a fractured toy I've grown tired of.
I am an outing I spoil with a tantrum.
I am a lost little scared little boy.

Mother and Father both are remarried.
Mother and Father throw us around.
Each has brand-new kids, live far from each other.
We have five new halfway sisters and brothers.
They have first dibs on our father and mother.

I am a weather-scarred football, forgotten.
I am away on my own now at college.
I am a scared little lost little boy.

Gertrude and I argue too much too often.
Gertrude and I think we're harming the kids.
Sometimes we feel that it's better to end it.

Other times, clinging, we won't concede defeat.
I cannot yield and make halfway connections.
I cannot give and take offers of peace.
Can't even handle pure, simple affection.
I am a lost little scared little boy.
I am a terrified lost little boy.

HOW WE CAME TO STAND ON THAT SHORE

Jay Rogoff

How we came to stand on that shore
I don't know, but in the failing
light whose particles sank in the sea
like diamonds, my father threw
his arm around me and walked me down
the beach. "The place was gorgeous then,"
he said, waving his free arm at
the shuttered mansions and concession
stands. "loved your mother then."
Tar and glass cluttered the beach.
A steaming smokestack looked stuck
in the ocean like a lipsticked
cigarette in a coffee cup.
                   Why
we came to walk on that shore I
don't know except
for him to say, as before, "You
are the best thing I have done."
He'd stopped and stood stopping me.
"I've never told you this." The light
had nearly gone. Waves crept in
like shark fins, dark against dark.
"When your mother and I vacationed
here, I know that there is where
you got started." I followed
his finger up to the boarded-up
window in the now burned-out hotel.

CUSTODY

Maureen Flannery

He has stretch marks on his back
as though the rack had pulled his arms
from their sockets and they dangled
on sinews of rubber band.
He is crucified outstretched
and the crossbeam reaches across town
where nails in too divergent households
try to pin him down.

MY MOTHER ATTENDS THE WEDDING OF MY DAUGHTER

Carole Peckham

My mother attends the wedding of my daughter
on September ninth.
I must spin a web against her,
Sitting in the corner, my old enemy,
Wrinkled and busy with her trouble.
For there against the fireplace,
Pale with an ancient beauty
Old as wedding days,
My daughter,
Her hair
Pulling, pulling that young stranger up.

The guests are my history:
Sisters,
Two shucked husbands
And the nice new one.
The attending in-laws,
Chidren grown
From old familiar sperm,
Friends who stuck it out
Through fractured vows,
My mother.

My first son and my daughter
Meet their half siblings,
Speak pleasantly to their father,
My first husband.
My third husband talks
To an old friend of my second marriage.
My first mother-in-law flirts

With an old lover,
Who, as it happens,
Is the father of my second husband.
And my second son from the second marriage
In funny conversation
With the second daughter from my
First husband's second marriage
Asks,
How are we stuck together?
Whose father do you have?
And what is in common here?
Me.

I am the mirror at the ceremony.
Or the window
Through which they look
To greet their past
For one sweet afternoon.
The long years loosen the fists of rage
Until they clasp here
At the nuptial place.
Flowers and song,
The bright light of summer
And babies,
Babies everywhere.
Babies in the womb,
In the arms,
Babies thinned out to five and ten,
To twenty-five and eighty.
Babies in the heart.

Does he still love me?
Was that promise real?
My, what a load of old shards.

Focus on my youngest son

Down from camp for the wedding,
Tomorrow to be gone again.
A small grief on which
To skate across
Those old and greater ones,
Or check the
daughter of my first husband's
Second wife.
Bobbed hair and a smile
To charm a grave.

But that witch woman
Wearing her wolf smile
To coat her baby mind
Worries me still.
She would kill
If she could.
Her face,
an armory of thought
Aimed at this new young man
While the reverend,
Whom no one knows,
Cants into a hidden microphone.
My sisters stand behind her chair,
Anxious to avoid
The crazy eyes.
My brother and my father
Are not here.
Men are grief or jokes
Her twisted smiles teach,
While my daughter stands
Watching her new man
By the mantle
A halo of flowers on
Her angel hair.

Forget this crowd of memories
eating hors d'oeuvres.
The good men, whose beds
I made black nests,
Are amiable as pets.
Forget remorse
And the deep harm
Done to them
And the babies
Now swinging their feet happily
As they chatter with new chums
Or shoving sweet cake into the new mate.
The wedding is a miracle of friendliness.
Remember, if anything, the cost.
A modern woman with three husbands
Pays.

Oh, my daughter,
May your own girl's wedding
have no multiple men
Or the confusion of genes
That witness some daft search for
A sexual grail.

What will my own gift be
Among the antique quilts,
The appliances,
Shiny and reliable as new friends,
And the glasses for wine and water fragile as light?
I will be a wall to the witch woman,
While you run toward thorns
Or seas,
Or more babies.
But, just in case,
It may be best if you are both blinded
And that there are no tears
To make you see.

EX

HER DAUGHTER'S FUTURE WEDDING

Nita Penfold

All she can think about
is being in the same room
as her ex-husband.
The knives on the table.

THE FOLDING

Andrea Potos

She wonders if he ever
thinks about her now, ten years after
she was his *wife* —
entertaining his clients with an hour's notice,
cooking a second dinner when he'd come home late;
all the errands and cleaning she did,
the many loads of laundry each week;
though she found peace in the folding —
burrowed in the corner of the couch,
in morning silence, with my sister and I at school,
the warm mounds of clothes before her
while she peeled through the layers of cotton
and acrylic that sparked with static, all his socks
that took so long to match,
the olive greens and light browns,
the dark blues and blacks, she'd hold them up
to the arched sunroom windows to make sure
the colors were the same; and then
there were always single socks left over —
she'd unfold nightgowns and trousers,
shirts and towels, to search for the strays
that might be clinging in the folds;
and sometimes she'd go back down to the basement —
like a blind woman reading Braille,
she'd reach her whole arm in the dryer still warm
from its labor and find the missing ones.
She'd carry everything then
up the hushed, carpeted stairs to the bedroom,
open his dresser drawers, lay them neatly down in rows,
pairing what she could of her life to his.

THOUGHTS ON THE
DEATH OF AN EX-HUSBAND

Stephanie Kaplan Cohen

My once love,
at the end
were you still
so angry?

The arithmetic
of our entanglement
is a fierce equation.
Three thousand days

we spent together.
You had ten thousand days
after me.

Ten thousand days
for breaths to cleanse
and ten thousand nights
for dreams to blur the edges.

I wish
that when you lay dying
if you gave a thought
to us

you smiled
and petted the memory
of what we had hoped
to become.

QUINCY, CALIFORNIA

Tony Gloeggler

The kind of town we stopped
for gas and asked directions
to that hillside inn ten years ago
when it rained and rained
and we stayed in bed, lost count
of the times we came and came —

kind of town you now live in
with your second husband, split-
level home, roadside mailbox

town you called from late last night
to tell me about the sharp pains,
the red shredded things
that dropped into the water
as you sat on the toilet
forty years old, wanting your first child.

HALF OF A CONVERSATION
WITH AN EX

Dancing Bear

Dead.

They've all been crushed.

This is pointless.

I never said that.

Because you don't either.

No.

This is what I have been talking about.

You have put words in my mouth, again.

Encouragement would have been nice.

This is pointless.

I will.

You will be fine.

Uh-huh.

No.

That's not a good idea.

I will not.

It always meant more to me.

You didn't care.

Please stop.

I wrote those when I felt that way.

INSTRUCTIONS
TO THE DEPARTING HUSBAND

Lynne Burris Butler

Take everything you will need
for your new life — the many
silences that hung like suits
in your orderly closets,
the reasons you tended carefully
as a garden. Continue to water
them. They will feed you all winter.
Take the past, which is obsolete,
a history written by liars,
a canvas you can paint over.
Abandon the guilt you wore
like shoes that pinched
but were too good to throw out.
Refuse to accept the scraps
of affection that still come
your way like misdirected letters
or unordered goods. Unpack
quickly. If the rooms seem
empty, fill the cabinets
with Swiss chocolate, fine wine,
more money. Bolt your door
against the static from yesterday.
Keep moving. Learn nothing.

LOREEN TELLS YOU
HOW TO GET AWAY WITH IT

Nita Penfold

You fly out of Boston, sitting on the runway for three hours because of severe thunderstorms, miss your connecting flight to Eugene and have to be put up in a hotel for the night in Seattle, Washington, then take the first flight out in the morning for Oregon to visit your pregnant daughter and her boyfriend, who keeps you up until one in the morning telling you about his life and why he loves your daughter; then in Eugene, you rent a car and drive for fourteen hours up through these mountains and over this eerie black crater that's as silent as you've ever heard the world, as silent as the end of civilization, as silent as death; then down through llama farms and even a trace of desert with wild sage and coyote, through Lewiston, Idaho, where it smells like the armpit of the universe, all the way to Moscow, Idaho, to visit your other daughter and her boyfriend, who won't look you in the eye when he speaks to you; and when you're minding your own business, just driving out of town, maybe slightly over the speed limit, thinking about what a good time you've had and how different your daughters' boyfriends are, as different as they themselves are, you just happen to run over your ex-husband and you are so startled you back up to see what happened, maybe only once.

CONVERSATION WITH AN EX

John Grey

Still smooth under the eyes,
blood nudging just enough color
to your cheeks.
Your body raised that skin well.
And the mouth, once kissed,
omits no detail from the past.

But sometimes you're talking
and I'm this satellite dish
pulling in programs from all
over the ionosphere,
none of them you.

Your daughter Kitty was
in a minor bathroom scrape,
your son graduates from
high school this year,
your husband was just promoted
to senior accountant
and something about an upcoming
trip to the Bahamas.
This was the program as listed
that I didn't see.

Somewhere, beyond this conversation,
I am holed up on my sofa,
television blazing,
hands dancing like Astaire
across the remote control.

I love you,
a subtitle warns
from the midriff
of a naked lover
in a foreign play.

Muriel Castanis, Sculpture, 1987; courtesy OK Harris Gallery, NYC

STARTING OVER

IN THE LAND
OF THE FORMERLY MARRIED

J. Kates

There are no virgins in this country.
Every woman sleeps with experience
and is the reluctant lover of complexity.
The blood that runs between their legs
is the blood of time.

I am a newcomer in these parts,
but I know a little of the language,
picking it up in phrases from the natives.
"Tonight the kids are with their father"
means I am welcome.

CHANGE OF ADDRESS

William Matthews

"It doesn't get much light," the real
estate agent allowed, and didn't say,
as Nora Joyce did of a flat James let,
"It's not a fit place to wash a rat in."

Figure a 50% divorce rate,
you've got one chance in two a sale
provokes another sale and maybe
two transactions after that,

a pyramid scheme for grief. The agent didn't
smirk, I'll hand her that. When I'm asleep
and my navel is like the calm bubble
in a carpenter's level, rage is safe,

the way animals in a zoo are safe,
a little skittish and depressed but safe,
and yes, a little off their feed but safe.
And the rat? The rat looks radiant.

PUTTING AWAY RINGS

Mary Scott

Friday afternoon, I have no business
bothering the harried teller at the bank
for access to my safe deposit box
but I do anyway, compelled to lay
my engagement ring and wedding band to rest
beside my mother's and my grandmother's sets.

I finger the gold, worn thin in spots, surrender
the rings to the satin jewelry case
where they jangle against the bands bequeathed
from my dead foremothers, three solitaires
nearly identical in size and clarity as though
women in my family never aspired to more brilliance.
The teller inserts the steel box into the vault
like a casket into a mausoleum, and I think
this is wrenching as burying any other love.

I know tonight I will give myself to another man,
the first after fourteen years of marriage.
Yielding and vulnerable as a virgin, I will listen
for the sound of gold rings clanking against metal,
resigned as a woman buried alive hearing
the last nail hammered in the lid of her coffin.

DIVORCEE

Linn Fiedler-Bourjeau

If my audacity or hair color shock you,
know that I too am surprised
that truths flame violet from my tongue,
that ideas glow red from my hair follicles,
for I was once a pale smile
waiting by some man's front door.
Leaping without a net
I found I could fly.
My feathers stick up at odd angles,
for tears wet unfurling wings
as I emerge from the birdcage of my ribs.

STARTING OVER

Louis McKee

After the divorce it took awhile
in a small cheap apartment,
but finally I got another house,
this one bigger, emptier.
I moved in with nothing
of my own to fill the rooms,
but still threw out the two chairs
and table the previous owners left.
I kept the doll I found
in the yard, a Barbie with matted
blonde hair and not a stitch
of clothing. A new wife,
I thought, and I proposed to her
right there in the middle
of my cutting grass, lifting
my beer in a toast to love
and long years together, and though
I doubt she really wanted it,
I did pour some on her hard pretty body,
and used my fingers to run away
the mud that was caked all over her.
Later I actually bathed her
in lemon-scented Joy, along with
the dish and glass I'd used for breakfast,
lunch and dinner.
                    I didn't feel weird

about any of this yet; this was still weeks
before I was in Kmart and bought
the outfit, jeans and a plaid flannel shirt,
Cowgirl Barbie, but for comfort, really,
something to wear about the house.
It would have been wrong if I'd gotten
the tight black sequined dress I saw,
or the hot baby blue mini with the silver
belt and matching fuck-me pumps.
It would have been wrong if I had
kept her naked, sitting on the bookcase
bare-assed for all the world to see.
But is this so wrong?

               She listens to me
sometimes; sometimes I can tell
she is not paying attention at all,
but that's okay; sometimes I'm not much
for talking myself. She is always there
when I need her, though. Is that so wrong?
And I'm always there for her.

               The yard
is her nightmare, but she knows I won't let
that happen to her again. I'm not so sure
about the life she's had, the station to which
she's been accustomed, but it is good here,
in this big empty house. She's treated well,
and her wardrobe, now, is next to none.

PATIENCE

Charles Fishman

If you're the woman I love,
why do I keep looking? As if
another could satisfy some need
you are blind to, as if her hand
might touch wounds that won't heal
in your presence.

She was the one I dared wait for:
late-night dream-walker, sister
and missing bone, dark mirror.
Blonde when I wanted blonde, wet
when my hand reached her, yes
to all my questions.

Yet I couldn't rise to her
expectations — I wasn't that gifted
in darkness, after all. I was no
wizard, no sorcerer. I loved
her body the way you might love
roses or a fine Victorian inkwell.

I wanted to dip myself into her
again and again, to write
the missing chapters of my life
in her body. But I couldn't
take her into my mind the way
you take me into your arms:

Wholly. Recklessly. Yielding
all pretense. With her,
I was naked but guarded: She
was a drug. Amoral. Un-
predictable. Inconstant.

She was a vision, and you
a splinter that nests in my heart.
You wound me, and I can't stop
taking you in. This is a blood
contract between us.

You are writing something inside
me with your sharp tongue,
with your loyal blood, with your
infinite patience. Some day,
your true faith tells you,
I will read what is etched there:

Rest, lover, you have no more to prove.

NECESSITIES

Mary Scott

After divorce,
my new condo
barely contains
everyone I love
and isn't large enough
to house my dejection.

First Easter alone,
my family gathers
around me for dinner.
Dad brings vegetables
from his garden and
a battered metal bucket
filled with pink roses
he cut that morning.

Overblown blooms
like rouged cheeks
distract me from
bleak surroundings.

This patriarchal blessing
brings to mind
his self-appointed tour
of my first apartment
twenty years ago.

Back then he inspected
the refrigerator for meat,
greens, fruit and milk,
pronounced it sufficient.
It was enough then,
to wish for his daughter.

But now he brings roses,
knowing I will be wanting,
wanting more than he can give.

OVER A DRINK
AT DORSHEID'S BAR

Nita Penfold

a man asks Loreen why women
always cut their hair
after they break up with a man.

Loreen could tell him
that

a woman who loses love
feels bad about herself,
wants a change;

she herself has gone
from long hair that she wore
as a shield, a protection
primly wrapped in a bun or
sometimes in a ponytail declaring
her flippant youthful outlook
to shorter layers that flew
all over her head in confusion
to razor-thin hair sticking
straight up to cut anyone
who got too close.

But that seems too esoteric,
so

Loreen explains that it's basically
so they won't attract
the same kind of jerk again.

MARGARITAS

T. Rochelle

Beri is the funniest girl in the world.
Kathy's been a little depressed.
Josie's just gotten off work
counseling rapists and pedophiles,
and because it is still the March
of my thirty-third birthday,
we're sitting on the patio of El Toro
drinking grade margaritas on a Tuesday night,
discussing the elusive concept of sober sex
while our waiter runs the chips-and-salsa
relay so he doesn't miss a word.
For Josie and me, newly single after a decade,
like planets slung off our axes,
and Kathy, of ruler-strict Catholic upbringing,
sex intrigues us like a foreign language.
But Beri, married for more than four years,
is having a hard time remembering sex at all,
its permutation of limbs, its wet rock and slide,
though she pretends, and she doesn't know I see
she's counting on her fingers under the table —
best I can figure, it was Christmas,
Charles's tired stocking stuffer
offered up like a diamond necklace.
Joe says it takes three martinis
to forget the day's fun accounts
of rodents and rectal thermometers.
Kathy needs five beers on an empty stomach
to get past god, his son, and the holy ghost,
and I'm thinking half a bottle
of a decent dry white, I'll relax a little

about the popped balloons of my breasts,
the post-Caesarean belly battle zone
my husband traded in for a twenty-year-old
with a moon-pie face and perky ta-tas.
The waiter smiles a young Spanish smile
that tells us he understands this English perfectly,
understands our need for extra sour cream,
and suddenly we're appreciating the fit of his apron
over tight black jeans, the neon sombrero
glow washing over our enchiladas,
the low night rumble of practical sedans
burrowing back to the suburbs
like guilty fathers, and the clear constant moon,
with its gathering of all things oozing and flowing,
that keeps us glued together. We've fallen
silent as the empty fishbowls
in which swim our dreams of love
in dregs of salt and citrus when Kathy says,
You have to really trust a man to have sober sex.

FEEDING THE WORMS

T. Rochelle

You think this is going to be a poem about death,
but it's really about being hungry all the time.
It's about craving sweets, even though I don't eat sugar
because of my past history of killing off
pound-bags of candy corn and wedding cookies
so I could puke them up like childhood shame
before my daily descent into a bottle.
It's about having kids when I knew better — three,
with a man who vanished into his Creole spices,
polished silver, jazz ringing the glassware,
and the slick smiles of young women ready to serve.
It's about a chafing cat-lick of a marriage
that eventually rubbed me raw, and the divorce,
a bad disease that started as a rash,
and later, a man who kisses me like I'm clean,
like there is nowhere else he wants to go.
It's about telling this man he needs to take Vermox
because at least one of my kids has pinworms,
and how, these days, I hang my head in the toilet
searching for shit for signs of parasites
as if they were the threads of my life unraveling
and I could stitch them back together again.
The whole family has to be treated, and I can't
figure out a way to tell him this
without implying he's part of the family.
And that might scare him away, the very thought
of being part of a family with worms,
with an eight-year-old who plays Boxcar Children
barefoot in the dirt, baking cakes
of grass and sticks, who pretends her father's dead,

that she could bear to lose her mother too.
Of part of a woman who's spent so much of her life
in the bathroom, on her knees. See,
this is not a poem about death, not yet,
but a love poem, my first.

THE WAY TO SURVIVE DIVORCE

Meg Campbell

The way to survive divorce
is with your hands.
Examine them. Speak to them.
Heed their reply.
Watch where they lead, and follow.
To the garden. To the kiln.
To the tiller on high seas.

Didn't they teach you to walk?
Dress rehearsal on knees,
scouts scurrying ahead?

You married with your hands.
Ring finger, all that.
Canada geese migrating south,
hands will lead you out.

Mine have. Pen in palm.
My mother's did.
Playing piano.
She dragged them like lumps of clay
to the keyboard in grief.
Pressing keys, they grew light and supple.
Night after night she played Broadway hits
and sang.
Slipping out from the weight of her pain
to the piano bar at La Valencia
or onboard a cruise ship
where music swirls with gaiety.

It was her hands
I see tonight.
At seventy-three, her fingers dart across keys,
nimbly bringing arms along.
Her shoulders lift with syncopated rhythm.
Seated at the piano bench,
feet tapping pedals and singing,
she is a passionate flamenco dancer
whirling castanets.
Unveiling her heart
with her hands.

About the Editors

MEG CAMPBELL is the author of *Solo Crossing* (Midmarch Arts Press, October 1999) a memoir in poems about her journey through separation and divorce to a new life. She is on the faculty at the Harvard Graduate School of Education and Executive Director of Expeditionary Learning Outward Bound. A graduate of Radcliffe College, she lives in Boston with her two daughters, Moriah and Adrienne.

WILLIAM DUKE is publisher of Poetry central.com and co-hosts a popular weekly poetry reading in Manhattan, The Saturn Series. He co-teaches a poetry immersion course with Meg Campbell at Teachers & Writers Collaborative and is working on his first book of poems, *Unwrapped.* He is a Dartmouth College graduate and works as a New Media consultant. He has two daughters, Isabel and Emily.

About the Artists

Artists Muriel Castanis, Marian Lerner Levine, Joan Semmel, and Lisa Zwerling all live in New York. Their works have been widely shown in galleries in the New York area and throughout the United States.

Typographic Design: Barbara Bergeron
Cover Design: MOG